Against All Opposition

other Walker books by Jim Haskins

Bill Cosby: America's Most Famous Father

Outward Dreams: Black Inventors and Their Inventions

Against All Opposition
Black Explorers in America

Jim Haskins

Walker and Company
New York

First published in the United States of America in 1992 by Walker Publishing Company, Inc.

Published simultaneously in Canada by Thomas Allen & Son Canada, Limited, Markham, Ontario.

Cataloging-in-Publication Data
Haskins, James, 1941–
Against all opposition: Black explorers in America / Jim Haskins.
p. cm.
Includes bibliographical references (p.) and index.
Summary: Surveys the lives and adventures of Black explorers who helped discover new worlds.
ISBN 0-8027-8137-3 (cloth). —ISBN 0-8027-8138-1 (reinforced)
1. Afro-American explorers—Biography—Juvenile literature.
2. Explorers, Black—Biography—Juvenile literature. 3. United States—Discovery and exploration—Juvenile literature.
4. Discoveries in geography—Juvenile literature. [1. Explorers.
2. Afro-Americans—Biography. 3. Discoveries in geography.]
I. Title.
E185.96.H353   1992
910′.08996—dc20   91-30203
CIP
AC

Text design R Studio T

Printed in the United States of America

4   6   8   10   9   7   5

t o

David

contents

acknowledgments   *ix*

chapter 1   *1*
Before Columbus

chapter 2   *7*
Estevanico and the Seven Cities of Gold

chapter 3   *15*
The Founding of Chicago

chapter 4   *24*
York and the Lewis and Clark Expedition

chapter 5   *31*
James P. Beckwourth, Rip-roaring Mountain Man

chapter 6   *40*
The Unknown Explorers

chapter 7   *46*
Matthew Henson at the Top of the World

chapter 8   62

*The Stars, My Goal: Guion Stewart
Bluford, Jr.*

chapter 9   72

Ronald McNair and the Challenger
Disaster

afterword   *81*

bibliography   *83*

index   *85*

acknowledgments

I am grateful to Anne Jordan, Ann Kalkhoff, and
Kathy Benson for their help. For assistance in
obtaining photographs, thanks are also
due to Emily Lewis.

chapter
1

BEFORE
COLUMBUS

*Great ideals are the glory of man alone. No other
creature can have them. Only man can get a
vision and an inspiration that will lift him above
the level of himself and send him forth against all
opposition or any discouragement to do and to
dare and to accomplish wonderful and great
things for humanity. . . . There can be no conquest to the man who dwells in the narrow and
small environment of a groveling life, and there
can be no vision to the man the horizon of whose
vision is limited by the bounds of self. But the
great things of the world, the great accomplish-
ments of the world, have been achieved by men
who had high ideals and who have received great
visions. The path is not easy, the climbing is
rugged and hard, but the glory at the end is
worthwhile.*

When Matthew Henson, the first black man to
reach the North Pole, spoke these words in
the early twentieth century, he was expressing

a credo held by all explorers of all races over the ages. There is something that excites the imagination when one is faced by the unknown, something that spurs humanity to risk life and limb to explore the unknown both within our world and, today, in the limitless expanse of the universe. And that need to know is not bound by color, sex, or nationality; it is only limited by the imagination.

Contrary to the portrait painted by most histories of the exploration of the world, blacks of all nationalities have made significant and lasting contributions in expanding the horizons of humanity. When contemplating discoveries, the names of Estevanico, Matthew Henson, or Guion Bluford might come to mind; but long before Estevanico set foot in what is now the southwestern United States, or Henson helped raise the flag at the North Pole, or Bluford leaped into space, black people had left their footprints in the soil of the Americas.

Africa was once the home of a number of great civilizations known for their wealth, technology, and learning. These civilizations were destroyed by the slave trade, but there is evidence that some of the first explorers of the New World came from the so-called Dark Continent and left their mark upon the New World long before Columbus made his discoveries.

"Fill two hundred ships with men. Fill another two hundred with water, food and gold; enough for two years," commanded the Emperor of Mali, "and do not return until you have reached the end of the ocean, or when you have exhausted your food and water."

Over two hundred years before Columbus set forth on his voyage of discovery, the empire of Mali blossomed on the western coast of Africa. Mali was more than prosperous, with gold one of its main items of trade. By the twelfth century, Mali's trade routes stretched north to Morocco and east to the Arabian countries. Mali's grand cities boasted an educated people, and their emperor was wealthy beyond imagining, according to Omari's *Masakil-al-absub* and the comments of one Abulfeda (1273–1332). This wealth and education spurred the Malians to look beyond the narrow boundaries of the known world and wonder what was to be found. So the Emperor of Mali commanded his people to outfit ships and venture forth across the Atlantic. A scholar and trader, Ibn Amir Hajib, later questioned the Emperor Kankun Musa of Mali about these explorations, which were ordered by Musa's predecessor:

> *The monarch who preceded me would not believe that it was impossible to discover the limits of the neighboring sea. He wished to know. He persisted in his plan. . . . [The commanders of the ships] went away and their absence was long: none came back, and their absence continued. Then a single ship returned. We asked the captain of their adventures and their news. He replied: Sultan, we sailed for a long while until we met with what seemed to be a river with a strong current flowing in the open sea. My ship was last. The others sailed on, but as each of them came to that place they did not come back nor did they reappear; and*

3

*I do not know what became of them. As for me, I
turned where I was and did not enter the current.*

It is conjectured that the "strong current" spoken
of by the captain of the remaining ship of the fleet
refers to the current at the mouth of the Amazon and
that the grand fleet of Mali had reached the coast of
South America. Nothing is known of what became of
the other ships in the vast fleet of discovery sent out by
the Emperor of Mali, but evidence exists that either
these explorers or other, earlier explorers from Africa
had an impact on civilizations in the New World. In
1975, graves and statues were discovered that led ar-
chaeologists to announce that Africans, rather than
Columbus or the Vikings, were the first overseas explorers to land in the New World, possibly as early as
4000 B.C. Statues with Negroid features have been
found at La Venta in Central America, and there are
paintings of black men in the murals of the Temple of
Warriors at Chichén Itzá. There are also similarities
between some of the languages of the Americas and
those of Africa.

In Europe, rumors circulated of explorations made
beyond the sea by the Norse, the Celts, and the Africans. It is certain that Columbus heard these rumors.
His son Ferdinand Colon wrote:

> *He took notice of what any persons whatsoever
> spoke to that purpose, and of sailors particularly,
> which might in any way be of help to him. Of all
> these things he made such good use that he con-*

4

The Olmec culture of Central America flourished from around 500 B.C. to about 1150 A.D. Statues that still stand at La Venta, in present-day Mexico, have distinctly Negroid features, suggesting to some scholars that Africans may have visited Central America long before Columbus. (New York Public Library Picture Collection)

*cluded for certain that there were many lands west
of the Canary Islands and Cape Verde, and that
it was possible to sail and discover them.*

Some historians claim that Columbus had a black African navigator on his initial voyage to the New World. One Pedro Alonzo Niño, who accompanied Columbus, is thought by some scholars to have been black. It is likely that Columbus had with him either black seamen or black slaves who had knowledge of the ocean and the lands beyond it.

Whether Columbus did or did not have a black navigator, he did have information gleaned from the explorations made by black Africans before the institution of slavery decimated the great civilizations of Africa, and his explorations did change the course of history in both the New and Old Worlds. One-half of the globe suddenly became open for exploration, and both white and black men and women sailed forth to find and claim this new land and increase the knowledge humanity had of its world.

chapter 2

ESTEVANICO AND
THE SEVEN CITIES
OF GOLD

S lavery has existed since before recorded time, but
it was not until the African slave trade developed
that slavery became a condition based upon the
color of a person's skin. The discovery of the New
World and the growth of the African slave trade went
hand-in-hand. By the sixteenth century the Europeans
had a new land—America—that needed manpower
for its development; Africa was a ready source of that
manpower. Companies grew up overnight to exploit
this living resource and to collect the enormous profits
that could be made.

The African slave trade can be said to have formally begun in 1441, when ten Africans were given to
Prince Henry of Portugal. This single action precipi-
tated a series of events that, for too long, have been

forgotten. Before the European exploitation of Africa, African culture and civilization matched and often surpassed that of Europe. The empire of Mali was not unique in Africa. The empire of Songhay in West Africa, which succeeded the Malian, enjoyed similar wealth and educational levels. Before Columbus discovered the New World, Leo Africanus, a Spanish Moor, visited Timbuktu in Songhay and noted a "great store of doctors, judges, priests, and other learned men, [and] . . . manuscripts or written books . . . which are sold for more money than any other merchandise."

With the development of the African slave trade, the art, music, culture, and knowledge of these civilizations were virtually erased and the black African relegated to the role of slave and servant to the white person. Yet, even in their condition of servitude, black Africans influenced the taming of the New World and left their mark upon the history of exploration. According to black poet Langston Hughes:

> *Negroes traveled with Columbus and, in 1513, thirty Negroes marched with Balboa to the Pacific and built the first ships on that coast. . . . The first wheat crop in the New World was planted and harvested by one of Cortez's black men. Negroes accompanied Pizarro in his conquest of Peru, and in 1565 they built St. Augustine, America's first city.*

In accompanying the various English, Spanish, and French explorations of the New World, black men made a significant contribution to increasing the

8

knowledge of these unknown lands. Because black people were held in low esteem and regarded only as slaves, most of the names of these intrepid explorers are lost to history. One name is remembered, however: Stephan Dorantez, known as Estevanico (?–1539).

Estevanico, or "Little Stephen," was born in the village of Azamer, near the Moroccan coast of Africa. The servant of Andres Dorantez de Carranze, Estevanico was chosen to accompany his master when Dorantez joined the six-hundred-man expedition of Pánfilo de Narváez to the New World to explore the northern shore of the Gulf of Mexico, seeking land and gold. On June 17, 1527, Estevanico and his master boarded a ship at Sanlúcar de Barrameda, Spain, and set sail for the New World.

The sea voyage was long and difficult and when the expedition at last landed in Santo Domingo to take on water and food, 143 men deserted. That was not the end of their troubles, however. More men were lost in a hurricane as they sailed to Cuba, and when at last the expedition reached the coast of Florida, on April 14, 1528, only four hundred remained.

Bad luck seemed to plague the small band of explorers. As they moved up the coast of Florida, they were beset by disease, which decimated their ranks, and then by the Florida Indians, who attacked and killed most of their party and enslaved the rest. Estevanico and the others were kept alive primarily due to Estevanico's skill with languages and the belief, on the part of the Indians, that he had the magical power to heal with his hands. Estevanico had a knowledge of medicine, acquired from the Moors, that he now put to good use among the Indians.

Finally escaping the Indians, Estevanico, Alvar Núñez Cabeza de Vaco, and the other survivors began a long and dangerous overland journey to Mexico City, where there was a Spanish settlement. Only four of them arrived in Mexico City in 1536, as De Vaco writes in his *The Journey of Alvar Núñez Cabeza de Vaco* in which he tells of how Estevanico saved his life with his skills in survival. The journey was arduous and Estevanico, as De Vaco notes, "was our go-between; he informed himself about the ways we wished to take, what towns there were, and the matters we desired to know." One result of this journey was that Estevanico became familiar with the geography of the country and with a number of Indian dialects, and, from the Indians, first heard the legend of the Seven Cities of Cíbola.

The search for gold had long motivated the Spaniards' exploration of the New World. When the Spanish in Mexico heard the rumors of the Seven Cities of Cíbola, their excitement could not be contained. Here, at last, must be the gold for which they had searched so long. Ceuolo or Cíbola was supposedly hidden somewhere in the American Southwest and was said to be fabulously rich in gold and other treasure. In 1539, Estevanico was leased by Antonio de Mendoza, then viceroy of Nueva España (New Spain—now Mexico), to serve as scout and to accompany Fray (Friar) Marcos de Niza, the leader of the expedition, in search of Cíbola.

Accompanied by a small band of Pima Indians, the two set off on March 7, 1539, from Culiacán, Mexico.

Estevanico was dressed to entice any Indians they might encounter: Records describe him as a lively and merry man who decorated himself with brilliant plumes and feathers. Little bells attached to his arms and legs tinkled with every movement. He carried a magical gourd decorated with red and white feathers. When it was borne in advance of the group by one of the Pima, the gourd was often accepted as a symbol of authority by the Indians.

So, with Estevanico dressed as a medicine man, the small expedition traveled north from Mexico City into the territory that is now New Mexico and Arizona, enduring great hardship and deprivation. Finally, in the Sonora Valley, Fray Marcos fell ill, but he sent Estevanico and four Indians on alone, arranging for Estevanico to send back crosses, whose sizes were to indicate the importance and size of the settlements the explorers encountered. As Fray Marcos wrote,

> *I sent Stephan Dorantz the Negro another way, whom I commaunded to goe directly northward fiftie or threescore leagues, to see if by that way hee might learne any newes of any notable thing which wee sought to discover, and I agreed with him, that if hee found any knowledge of any peopled and riche Countrey which were of great importance, that hee should goe no further, but should returne in person, or shoulde sende mee certaine Indians with that token which wee were agreed upon, to wit, that if it were but a meane thing, hee should sende mee a White Crosse of one handfull long; and if it were any great matter,*

*Q*uetzalcoatl is the feathered serpent of ancient Mexican mythology. Some scholars believe that the idea of a giant feathered serpent may have been brought to Central America from Africa. (New York Public Library Picture Collection)

one of two handfuls long; and if it were a Coun-
trey greater and better than Nueva Espanna, he
should send mee a great crosse . . . and within
foure dayes after the messengers of Stephan
returned unto me with a great Crosse as high as a
man, and they brought me word from Stephan,
that I should forthwith come away after him, for
hee had found people which gave him information
of a very mighty Province, and that he had sent
me one of the said Indians. This Indian told me,
that it was thirtie dayes journey from the Towne
where Stephan was, unto the first Citie of the sayd
Province, which is called Ceuola. Hee affirmed
also that there are seven great Cities in this
Province, all under one Lord, the houses whereof
are made of Lyme and Stone, and are very great.

Excited by the news, Fray Marcos set out to join
Estevanico, but three days before he reached the area
where Estevanico was supposed to be, Estevanico's
Indian messengers, bloody and wounded by arrows,
staggered into Fray Marcos' camp with the news that
Estevanico was dead. They told Fray Marcos that Estevanico had sent a token of peace to the local leader
of the city he had found. Instead of honoring the
peace token, the leader had refused it and had taken
Estevanico prisoner and put him into a house without
food or drink. They refused to meet with him and

they took from Stephan all the things which hee
carried with him. The next day when the Sunne
was a lance high, Stephan went out of the house
and saw a crowd of people coming at him from

13

the city whom as soone as hee sawe he began
to run away and we likewise, and foorthwith they
shot at us and wounded us, and certain men fell
dead upon us . . . and after this we could not see
Stephan any more, and we thinke they have shot
him to death, as they have done all the rest which
went with him, so that none are escaped but we
only.

So reported the nineteenth-century historian Richard Hakluyt.

With the death of Estevanico, Fray Marcos and his band turned back to Mexico City. The Spanish, yet again, had not found the legendary gold they sought, although Estevanico's exploits were to spur the later searches for Cíbola by Coronado.

To this day, the legend of Cíbola, the fabulous Seven Cities of Gold, persists, although many historians speculate that what Estevanico had found in the arid Southwest were the pueblo settlements of the Zuñis. The memory of Estevanico lingers on, however, in Indian legends of a black "Mexican" who traveled among the Indians long ago and who was slain. What remains as fact rather than legend is that Estevanico, Stephan Dorantez, was one of the first explorers of what is now the western United States.

chapter
3

THE FOUNDING
OF CHICAGO

*T*he seventeenth and eighteenth centuries saw a
tide of immigrants flowing into the New World,
all eager to exploit the land, the freedom it
offered, and the resources and opportunities inherent
in the untamed wilderness. Black and white alike came
to start new lives but, while most of the white men
and women came freely to the shores of the New
World, the black men and women were, too often,
dragged there in chains as slaves or indentured
servants.

By 1700, the east coast of colonial America blossomed with towns and cities. Farms sprang up, and the
wilderness was beaten back. Yet, beyond the area of
what is now western Pennsylvania, the land was still
unconquered—and largely unexplored, except by lone,
intrepid men who roamed it trapping for furs or trad-

ing with the Indians. One such explorer was a free black man who had come voluntarily to America to seek his fortune. He was to leave behind him a monument that persists today, although for many years his contribution to the exploration and settling of America went unrecognized. That man was Jean Baptiste Point du Sable; his monument, the city of Chicago.

Jean was born in St. Marc, Haiti, around 1750, and was of mixed French and Negro parentage. For a time his father had been a pirate roaming the Caribbean, swooping down in his ship upon the various islands' small settlements and upon other ships to raid and plunder. Jean's mother, Suzanne, was a slave on a Danish plantation on the island of St. Croix when his father raided that island. He took Suzanne with him and carried her to Haiti, where she was free.

When Jean was ten years old, his mother died. Faced with the responsibility of a young boy to raise, Jean's father gave up the perilous life of a pirate and became a respectable merchant. He took Jean to France and placed him in a good school near Paris. It was here that Jean met Jacques Clemorgan of Martinique, who was to become a lifelong friend and accompany him on many of his later adventures.

When Jean returned to Haiti from France, he had grown into a handsome, educated young man. For a few years he worked in his father's business but, like so many other young men through the ages, he grew bored with it and yearned for adventure, excitement, and fortune. His father understood Jean's feelings; those same stirrings had spurred him to become a pirate in his own youth. So he encouraged Jean Baptiste to strike out on his own. He gave Jean his own ship, named *Suzanne,* and, with his friend Jacques Clemorgan, Jean set out to seek his fortune in America, heading for New Orleans, in the French colony of Louisiana.

The two young men began their journey with high hopes, but from the beginning their travels seemed fated for ill fortune. Both Jean and Jacques had grown up on the ocean and knew the seas and sailing as well as they knew how to walk and talk; but all their knowledge and experience were no match for a hurricane. Buffeted by raging winds and beaten by towering waves, the *Suzanne* was dashed to pieces in the storm. The two young men were rescued and taken to New Orleans, but once there they encountered further difficulties because of their color.

New Orleans in the mid-1700s was one of the main ports for the slave trade. To be black and walking about freely was to be automatically suspected of being a runaway slave. Nor were there jobs available to a free black person in such a society. Fearful of being mistaken for runaway slaves and faced with the prospect of no work, Jean and Jacques hid for a while with a group of Jesuits and made plans. They decided to travel farther north, where it was safer for them and where they might find a life without the threat of slavery. They agreed to journey up the Mississippi River, trapping for furs and trading with the Indians.

Once they set out, it seemed their bad luck was over. They slowly made their way upriver, trapping and trading, finally stopping at St. Louis, where they set up a thriving business trading with the Indians. In 1767, however, the city came under British control, and Jean was forced to leave.

The French and Indian Wars (1754–1763) had been settled by the Treaty of Paris in 1763, but those who were sympathetic to the French or to the Indians were still suspect in the eyes of the British even four years later. Jean's French background and his close ties with the Indians made him an immediate suspect. To avoid the threat of imprisonment, he moved farther north into Illinois territory, settling among the Peoria and Potowatomi Indians. It was among the Potowatomi that he found his wife, a beautiful Indian girl named Kittihawa ("Fleet of Foot").

Although it was not until 1788 that Jean Baptiste and Kittihawa—or Catherine, as she was also then called—were married before a Catholic priest at Cahokia, Illinois, Jean had married Kittihawa in an Indian ceremony in 1764. Jean became a member of Kittihawa's tribe and, initially, settled down near Fort Peoria, where their first child, a son, was born. However, Jean Baptiste was not one to sit quietly and watch the grass grow after a life of travel and adventure. In 1769, wanderlust again struck and he was off once more to explore new territories.

He traveled north to Canada, following the Illinois River and Lake Michigan, trapping and trading. Using this route, Jean stopped at the main portage point between the river and Lake Michigan, an unpleasant, swampy area called by the Indians Eschikagou. He

realized the importance of the area to any travel northward and, in 1772, after returning to Fort Peoria, he
told Kittihawa that he meant to return there and set up
a trading post.

In 1774, Jean, Kittihawa, and their son led Kittihawa's clan northward and erected the first buildings at
Eschikagou. The house Jean built for his family, which
initially served also as his trading post, was no rude
affair. It had five rooms and a fireplace and measured
twenty-two feet by forty feet. As the trading post grew,
he also built a bake house, a dairy, a poultry house, a
smokehouse for curing meats, a stable, a workshop,
and a mill powered by horses. The other members of
the clan also built houses, quickly establishing a busy,
prosperous settlement. To add to it, Kittihawa gave
birth to a daughter, Suzanne, named for Jean's mother.
Suzanne was the first child born in what is now the city
of Chicago.

Jean Baptiste's settlement prospered and grew.
Travelers and settlers passing through often chose to
stop there, staying permanently. The little trading
community expanded and soon became known as the
best trading post between St. Louis and Montreal. Just
when things seemed perfect, however, the same problem that had forced Jean to flee St. Louis cropped up
again.

The British could not believe Jean was not a French
spy; he spoke French fluently, had lived for a time in
France, and he traveled freely among the Indians.
In 1778, the English commander of the area arrested
him for "treasonable intercourse with the enemy,"

*B*orn free in Haiti, Jean Baptiste Point du Sable became a successful fur trader and explorer along the Illinois River and Lake Michigan. He built the first settlement at the site of present-day Chicago. (Chicago Historical Society)

describing him at the time as a "handsome Negro, well educated and settled at Eschikagou, but [who] was much in the interest of the French."

Jean was taken to Fort Mackinac in what is now Michigan, where he remained for a year before being released. Although he was technically a prisoner, the British treated him well, trusting him enough to allow him to hunt and fish around the fort. He was described in an official report as having "in every way behaved in a manner becoming to a man of his station, [with] many friends who give him a good character." Since no charges were ever filed against him, the British released him in 1779 and Jean returned to his trading post.

For the next ten years, Chicago continued to grow and Jean's business prospered. In 1800, however, Jean began to feel his age and decided it was time to retire from the strenuous life of a trapper and trader. He drew up papers and sold all his holdings in Chicago to a man named John Lalime for twelve hundred dollars.

Jean's wealth at that time is reflected in the partial inventory of his home done when the sale was completed. It included one large cabinet with glass doors, one bureau, four tables, seven chairs, one large feather bed, one couch, a stove, a score of large wooden dishes, four tin basins and three pewter basins, a churn, one iron coffee mill, one pair of scales with weights, eleven copper bottles, two copper bells, one tin lantern, one leather and one metal wire sack, one toasting iron, two mirrors, two pictures, one hatchet, and four planes, plus a bag of carpenter's tools. Although by modern standards this list seems paltry, it includes items that were considered luxuries at the time, such as the cabinet with glass doors and the two mirrors, when most people had none.

The sale was witnessed by a man named John Kinzie, who then carried the bill of sale to St. Joseph, Michigan, for filing. Because of his willingness to assist at the sale, Kinzie ironically created a confusion that was to last well into the twentieth century.

In 1804, Kinzie decided to settle in Chicago himself. Because he was involved in the sale of Jean's trading post and because he himself lived in Chicago, Kinzie was credited erroneously for many years afterwards with the founding of the settlement of Chicago, despite the fact that, until 1927, a plaque existed crediting the founding of Chicago to "Jean Baptiste Point De [sic] Sable, a Negro from Santo Domingo . . ."

After the sale of his holdings, Jean and his family moved back to Peoria, where he owned eight hundred acres of land. There he remained until the death of Kittihawa in 1809. With Kittihawa gone, Jean moved southward to St. Charles, Missouri, where his son lived and where he remained until his death on August 28, 1818. He was buried in St. Borromeo Cemetery in St. Charles.

For the next 150 years, Jean Baptiste Point du Sable's contribution to the settlement of America went unacknowledged. In 1968, however, Du Sable's founding of the city of Chicago was formally recognized and a stone naming him as founder was placed upon his grave.

What had aided Jean Baptiste du Sable in his

adventures and explorations was the friendliness of the Indians toward black people. In many ways the Indians felt that they shared with the blacks a common enemy, the white man, and so they extended friendship and sympathy to black people. This empathy between the two was to aid in the further exploration and development of what would become the United States of America.

chapter
4

YORK AND THE
LEWIS AND CLARK
EXPEDITION

*I*n 1800, the land stretching between the Mississippi River and the Pacific Ocean was an unknown treasure box waiting to be opened. Even before he was elected president, Thomas Jefferson recognized the potential of these lands and dreamed of a nation—the United States—one day spanning the continent from the Atlantic to the Pacific. When he became secretary of state, Jefferson proposed that the government send an expedition to explore this territory. It was not until he assumed the presidency, however, that he was able to set such plans in motion. To head the expedition, Jefferson called upon his private secretary, Captain Meriwether Lewis. By 1803, Jefferson's dream had become reality and he was able to write to Lewis, "The object of your mission is to explore the Missouri river,

& such principle stream of it, as, by it's course & communication with the waters of the Pacific Ocean, may offer the most direct & practicable water communication across this continent, for the purposes of commerce."

In addition to discovering an accessible route to the Pacific, Lewis was also charged with describing the people whom the expedition might meet, the geographical features of the lands explored, mineral deposits, types of animals, and the weather—basically everything that the explorers might encounter. Thus was set into motion one of the most famous exploration expeditions in American history.

On June 19, 1803, after making elaborate preparations, Lewis wrote to William Clark, a long-time personal and professional friend, inviting him to join the expedition as coleader, saying, "If therefore there is anything . . . in this enterprise, which would induce you to participate with me in it's fatiegues, it's dangers and it's honors, believe me there is no man on earth with whom I should feel equal pleasure in sharing them as with yourself."

On July 29, Clark's reply reached Lewis in Pittsburgh as he headed west. Clark was delighted: "My friend I do assure you no man lives with whome I would perfur to undertake Such a Trip &c. as your self."

So, in October of 1803, William Clark joined Meriwether Lewis somewhere along the Ohio River, bringing with him a group of his own men.

The names of Lewis and Clark, and of the Sho-

shone Indian woman Sacajawea, who served as both guide and interpreter, are most frequently mentioned in discussions of the exploration of the American northwest. Yet there was another important member of that famous expedition of forty-four people who has been all but forgotten with the passage of time: York, Clark's slave and personal servant. It is doubtful whether, without York, Lewis and Clark would have enjoyed such friendly relationships with the Indian tribes along the way, or have achieved all they did in their explorations.

Little is known of York's background. Presumably he was a slave on the Clark farm in Virginia or was purchased in Kentucky, where the Clark family had moved in 1784 after the American Revolution. By 1803, however, York was Clark's personal servant and was deeply devoted to him.

According to Clark's diary, York was over six feet tall and weighed more than two hundred pounds—a prodigious size at that time, when the average man was significantly shorter and slighter than today. Because of his size and color, the Indians the expedition encountered were fascinated by him. York provided a means of entry into many Indian villages because of the Indians' curiosity. And because of his outgoing nature and sense of humor, York encouraged the Indians' curiosity with various antics. Among one tribe, Clark noted in his diary, "I ordered my black Servant to Dance which amused the crowd very much, and Somewhat astonished them, that So large a man should be active &c.,&c."

Most of the Indians had never seen or even heard of a black person before. They thought York's coloring must be paint and often tried to wipe it off. As one Flathead Indian reported of the Lewis and Clark expedition:

One of the strange men was black. He had painted himself in charcoal, my people thought. In those days it was the custom for warriors, when returning home from battle, to prepare themselves before reaching camp. Those who had been brave and fearless, the victorious ones in battle, painted themselves in charcoal. So the black man, they thought, had been the bravest of his party.

It is ironic that the man most respected by the Indians had the lowest status in the expedition.

York played up to this interest, telling the Indians, through an interpreter, tall tales about himself. As Clark wrote, "By way of amusement he told them that he had once been a wild animal, and caught, and tamed by his master; and to convince them showed them feats of strength which, added to his looks, made him more terrible than we wished him to be." And among the Indians of the Lolo Pass, Lewis wrote in his journal that York "had excited their curiosity very much. And they seemed quite as anxious to see this monster as they were the merchandize which we had to barter for their horses."

While York was an enormous help in overcoming the shyness or hostility of the Indian tribes that the expedition met, he was also a major asset in its daily

27

*T*he slave and personal servant of William Clark, York
accompanied Lewis and Clark on their search for a route
to the Pacific. His size and skin color fascinated the Indians
the expedition encountered, and he helped overcome their
hostility. He also demonstrated great bravery during the long
journey. When it was over, Clark freed him. ("York" by
Charles M. Russell. Montana Historical Society. Gift of the
Artist)

travels. The journey was arduous in the extreme, and fraught with dangers. In addition to being a skillful shot and providing the group with fresh meat, York was unquestionably brave.

The Missouri River, the expedition's main route of travel, was swift and dangerous, filled with currents and eddies that could quickly capsize a boat and sweep it and its crew away. At a point on the Missouri known as the Devil's Race Ground, one of the boats in the expedition lost control, heeling this way and that in the rushing waters and threatening to capsize and break to pieces. A number of brave men, York among them, jumped from the floundering boat and swam through the turbulent waters to carry a rope to those on shore so the boat could be controlled and pulled in, saving those who remained on board.

On November 7, 1805, after many such adventures, the expedition came to what they thought was the Pacific Ocean. It was, in fact, Gray's Harbor; the ocean itself was twenty miles farther on. The elation of the group, however, was unrestrained. Clark wrote: "Great joy in camp. We are in *view* of the *Ocian* . . . the great Pacific Octean which we have been so long anxious to See, and the roreing or noise made by the waves brakeing on the rockey Shore (as I suppose) may be heard distinctly."

It was not until November 18, however, when over a week had passed, that Clark led a small group of men, York among them, from their camp on Baker's Bay to the shore for a view of the great Pacific Ocean. Several weeks later, Clark immortalized their accomplishment, carving on a tree, "CAPT. WILLIAM CLARK DECEMBER 3RD 1805. BY LAND. U.STATES IN 1804–5."

Although the explorers had achieved their goal— the Pacific Ocean—their journey was hardly done. It would take another year for the hardy band to return to their starting point of St. Louis. Lewis and part of the group retraced their steps along the Missouri while Clark, York, and the remainder of the expedition went south along the Yellowstone River, the two groups reuniting on the Missouri on August 12, 1806. On September 2, 1806, Lewis wrote to President Jefferson from St. Louis, announcing the expedition's safe arrival there:

> *In obedience to your orders we have penitrated the continent of North America to the Pacific Ocean, and sufficiently explored the interior of the country to affirm with confidence that we have discovered the most practicable rout which does exist across the continent by means of the navigable branches of the Missouri and Columbia Rivers.*

Sometime after their return, Clark granted York his freedom, grateful for his help and support during the expedition. Nothing is known of York's life after leaving Clark. However, one story is that he immediately returned west and became the chief of an Indian tribe. Whether he became an Indian chief or not, York had already made his mark—although long unrecognized—on American history and assured his place in the annals of exploration of the North American continent.

chapter 5

JAMES P. BECKWOURTH, RIP-ROARING MOUNTAIN MAN

*A*fter the explorations by the Lewis and Clark expedition in the first decade of the nineteenth century, more and more people ventured west, some to settle on farms away from the cities, some to hunt and trap for furs, some to escape the fist of slavery. One such man was James P. Beckwourth (1798–1867) who was to become the most famous Indian fighter of his generation, and who, in his explorations, would open the West to countless settlers.

James P. Beckwourth was born in Virginia to a white man and a black slave woman. His father served as an officer in the Revolutionary War and, after the war, in the early 1800s, Beckwourth and his family, which included thirteen children, moved west, settling near St. Louis, Missouri. When son James was nineteen

years old, his father apprenticed him to a local black-
smith, a huge brute of a man who worked James hard
and who, gradually, began to enslave the young man.
When the man told James that he would not be permitted to leave in the evening after work or do as he
pleased in his free time, James became enraged and hit
the man. After that, he couldn't stay, for he could have
been hanged. He ran away, first going south to New
Orleans.

Finding no opportunities in New Orleans and, like
Jean Baptiste Point du Sable, seeing his freedom threat-
ened yet again in this center for the slave trade, James
Beckwourth returned to St. Louis and signed on in
1823 as a scout for General William Henry Ashley's
Rocky Mountain Fur Company.

The 1820s and 1830s were the heyday of the fur
trade and of loud, bragging mountain men, and young
Beckwourth fitted in naturally. As General William
Tecumseh Sherman was to say in 1848, "Jim Beckwourth . . . was, in my estimate, one of the best chroni-
clers of events on the plains that I have encountered,
though his reputation for veracity was not good."
Beckwourth loved a tall tale as well as anyone else and
was not above embellishing his adventures to make
them more interesting—not that the real adventures
themselves needed embellishment.

It was not unusual for an exploration or trapping
expedition to hire blacks as scouts and interpreters.
Colonel James Stevenson noted in 1888 that "the old
fur traders always got a Negro if possible to negotiate

for them with the Indians, because of their 'pacifying effect.' They could manage them better than the white men, with less friction." So Beckwourth was hired by Ashley.

While working for Ashley, Beckwourth became familiar with the plains west of St. Louis and with the Indian tribes inhabiting them. He also became proficient with a gun, bowie knife, and tomahawk. Having learned all he could after a year with the Rocky Mountain Fur Company, he resigned and struck out on his own, roaming the plains, trapping, and dealing with the Indians. A chance encounter with the Crow Indians in 1824 would lead, eventually, to Beckwourth's becoming an Indian chief.

James Beckwourth was respected by the Indians because he was a fair trader, but more so for his daring adventures and fierce nature; he was a short-tempered man who never backed away from a fight. On one of his visits with the Crow Indians in 1824, an old squaw declared he was her long-lost son. "What could I do under the circumstances," Beckwourth wrote in his autobiography. "Even if I should deny my Crow origin, they would not let me." He was adopted by the Crow and given the name "Morning Star." He soon married the chief's daughter (his third wife, according to some historians) and quickly rose to be chief himself.

Life with the Crow Indians was not peaceful, nor would a peaceful life have suited Beckwourth. He eagerly joined the Crow in their raids against the Blackfoot Indians and soon was known among the Crow as

*B*orn a slave in Virginia, James Beckwourth escaped and
headed west. He learned hunting, fishing, and trapping
from the Indians and lived with both the Crow and Blackfeet.
He once spent six years living with the Crow. (Mary O'H.
Williamson Collection, Prints and Photographs Department,
Moorland—Spingarn Research Center, Howard University)

Bloody Arm, because of his ferocity in battle. A Dakota Indian, Paul Dorion, described one battle Beckwourth engaged in:

> *"You are all fools and old women," he [Beck-wourth] said to the Crows; "come with me, if any of you are brave enough, and I will show you how to fight.*
>
> *He threw off his trapper's frock of buckskin and stripped himself naked like the Indians themselves. He left his rifle on the ground, took in his hand a small light hatchet, and ran over the prairie to the right, concealed by a hollow from the eyes of the Blackfeet. Then, climbing up the rocks, he gained the top of the precipice behind them. Forty or fifty young Crow warriors followed him. By the cries and whoops that rose from below he knew that the Blackfeet were just beneath him; and running forward he leaped down the rock into the midst of them. As he fell he caught one by the long loose hair, and dragging him down tomahawked him; then grasping another by the belt at his waist, he struck him also a stunning blow, and, gaining his feet, shouted the Crow war-cry. He swung his hatchet so fiercely around him, that the astonished Blackfeet bore back and gave him room. He might, had he chosen, have leaped over the breastwork and escaped; but this was not necessary, for with develish yells the Crow warriors came dropping in quick succession over the rock among their enemies. The main body of the Crows, too, answered the cry from the front, and rushed up simultaneously. The convulsive struggle within the breastwork was frightful; for*

*an instant the Blackfeet fought and yelled like
pent-up tigers; but the butchery was soon com-
plete, and the mangled bodies lay piled together
under the precipice. Not a Blackfoot made his
escape.*

By the 1840s, James Beckwourth had become a
legend, ranking alongside his friends Jim Bridger and
Kit Carson. But even the adventurous, warlike life with
the Crow couldn't hold him long, and he soon resumed
his wandering ways. Beckwourth took on the job as
army scout during the Second Seminole War in Florida, where he picked up a Spanish wife. The year 1844
saw him in California fighting alongside General Stephen Kearny in putting down California's Bear Flag
Revolt, its war for independence. Kearny had asked
Beckwourth to join, saying, "You like war, and I have
good use for you now." It was not until 1850, however,
that Beckwourth made the discovery that has preserved
his name for future generations.

In 1848, James Beckwourth became the chief scout
for John C. Frémont's expedition across the Sierra
Nevada Mountains. In April of 1850, Beckwourth
discovered a pass through the mountains, a pass that
was to become important during and after the gold
rush to California. As he wrote,

*It was the latter end of April when we entered
upon an extensive valley at the northwest extrem-
ity of the Sierra range. . . . Swarms of wild geese
and ducks were swimming on the surface of the
cool crystal stream, which was the central fork of*

*J*ames Beckwourth discovered a pass through the Sierra Nevada Mountains. It is known today as Beckwourth Pass. (Mary O'H. Williamson Collection, Prints and Photographs Department, Moorland—Spingarn Research Center, Howard University)

*the Rio de las Plumas, or sailed the air in clouds
over our heads. Deer and antelope filled the
plains. . . . We struck across this beautiful valley
to the waters of the Yuba, from thence to the
waters of the Truchy. . . . This, I at once saw,
would afford the best wagon-road into the American Valley approaching from the eastward, and I
imparted my views to three of my companions in
whose judgement I placed the most confidence.
They thought highly of the discovery, and even
proposed to associate with me in opening the
road. We also found gold, but not in sufficient
quantity to warrant our working it. . . .*

*On my return to the American Valley, I made
known my discovry to a Mr. Turner, proprietor of
the American Ranch, who entered enthusiastically
into my views; it was a thing, he said, he had
never dreamed of before. If I could but carry out
my plan, and divert travel onto that road, he
thought I should be a made man for life. There-
upon he drew up a subscription-list, setting forth
the merits of the project, and showing how the
road could be made practicable to Bidwell's Bar,
and thence to Marysville. . . . He headed the
subscription with two hundred dollars. . . .*

*In the spring of 1852 I established myself in
Beckwourth Valley, and finally found myself
transformed into a hotel-keeper and chief of a
trading-post. My house is considered the emi-
grant's landing-place, as it is the first ranch he
arrives at in the golden state, and is the only
house between this point and Salt Lake.*

James Beckwourth seemed set for life, profitably
running a hotel and trading post at the pass that bore

his name. He was not, however, fated to end his life as a "hotel-keeper." In 1859, he himself joined the California gold rush, and in 1864, he fought in the Cheyenne-Arapaho War. In 1867, the government asked him to go on a peace mission to his adopted tribe, the Crow. While he was there, according to one legend, the Crows asked Beckwourth to a tribal feast and once again tried to convince him to become their chief. When he refused, they poisoned him. William Katz reports in *Eyewitness: The Negro in American History:* "According to this version of his death, if the Crows could not have him as a live chief, they intended to keep Beckwourth in the tribal burial ground." Even James Beckwourth's death is surrounded by the aura of legend and tall-tale telling that characterized his life.

While James P. Beckwourth's adventures ranked with those of white mountain men and frontiersmen such as Kit Carson and Daniel Boone, he has been largely forgotten by historians of the frontier West. Even his biographer, while detailing his life, omits any mention of the fact that he was black. His name, however, lives on in the pass he discovered over the Sierra Nevada Mountains, northwest of what is today Reno, Nevada.

chapter
6

THE UNKNOWN

EXPLORERS

D uring the 1800s, most of the vast, green North American continent still awaited exploration and settlement by those who had traveled from distant shores. While small towns and settlements were scattered sparsely throughout the lands west of the Mississippi, it would be decades before the bustling cities of today emerged from the plains and mountains. After the middle of the century, the trickle of settlers to the West would become a river and then a flood.

While many people were venturing into the plains and west beyond the Rocky Mountains to seek their fortunes, in the eastern part of the United States a tumult was building that would erupt, in 1861, in the Civil War. Both before and after that war, blacks who had been enslaved or otherwise denied life's opportunities fled west to the lands free of oppression, there to explore, discover, and settle. Often they joined Indian tribes sympathetic to their plight or established their own communities. Quite a number of black men, although it is not mentioned in most histories, became cowboys or, like James Beckwourth, were mountain men and trappers and traders. But because the land was new to them, *anyone* venturing into the west, whether black or white, was in reality an explorer, unrecognized and, for the most part, forgotten.

This was also true of the Spanish territories in what is now the state of Florida. In the 1700s and 1800s, blacks knew more about the topography and geography of Florida than most white men did. Since Florida was a Spanish colony until 1819, hundreds of blacks fled their enslavement in the United States to settle there, where they were free. Many established whole communities in the forests and swamps of Florida, turning the fertile land into farms. A Colonel Clinch of the U.S. Army reported in 1816: "Their corn fields extended nearly fifty miles up the [Appalachicola] river and their numbers were daily increasing."

An equal number of fugitives chose to join with the Seminole Indians of Florida. So many, in fact, that America's first Indian treaty, in 1790, demanded that the Seminoles turn over the blacks who had come to share their lives. The Seminoles, however, refused; these people had become members of their tribe.

Increasingly, Florida was a thorn in the side of the United States. This led eventually to Spain's sale of Florida to the United States, and to three Seminole

Wars, all to stop the flow of slaves into Florida. As General Thomas Jesup said in 1836, of the Second Seminole War, "This, you may be assured, is a Negro, not an Indian War." At the close of this war, in 1842, the majority of Seminoles, with their black fellow tribe members, were moved to Oklahoma by the government.

What the government almost totally ignored before and after the conflict in Florida was the valuable knowledge of this area that had been gained by both blacks and Indians. Nearly one hundred years of working, living, and traveling throughout Florida was lost: navigation ways through swamps and knowledge of the geography of the land and its dangers and predators. All this experience was disregarded for the sake of one "peculiar institution"—slavery—an institution the Civil War would soon destroy.

In the western regions of America, lone explorers or small groups of blacks traveled the plains and mountains, also seeking freedom and land on which to settle. However, except when an individual was hired as a scout for a white expedition, any discoveries made have been largely forgotten, although one man is still occasionally remembered: George W. Bush.

In 1844, the Oregon territory was sparsely settled and was the subject of dispute between the Americans who had settled there and the great Hudson Bay Company of Great Britain. In spite of the dispute, one law had been agreed upon by all: Blacks were forbidden to settle there. In that same year, however, a small wagon train of both black and white settlers began a journey from Missouri, bound for the Oregon territories. Leading them was George W. Bush, a black man, accompanied by his wife and five children.

Little is known of George Bush's early life. As a young man, he had served bravely under Andrew Jackson during the 1815 Battle of New Orleans. After the Revolutionary War he had married and settled in Missouri, becoming wealthy from trading cattle. Why he decided to give up a comfortable and lucrative life in Missouri and go west is unknown. One might speculate that the increased tension about slavery—stemming initially from the Missouri Compromise of 1820 and strengthened by growing antislavery sentiments—may have forced Bush to a decision. A wealthy, free black man in a slave state, as Missouri was, may have found himself unwelcome and his—and his children's—opportunities increasingly limited.

Whatever his reasons, George Bush packed up his family and sought others to accompany them on their journey west. Because of his wealth, he was able to give financial help to a number of families who otherwise might not have been able to afford the trip. In 1844, with his good friend Michael T. Simmons, an Irish immigrant, Bush led his band west.

Because of his color, Bush was concerned about his welcome in the new territories and decided to settle north of the Columbia River because the territory south of the river had passed legislation banning black settlers. Another friend, John Minton, wrote:

> *I struck the road again in advance of my friends*
> *near Soda Springs. There was in sight, however,*

*G. W. Bush, at whose camp table Rees [Minton's
traveling companion] and I had received the
hospitalities of the Missouri rendezvous. Joining
him, we went on to the Springs. Bush was a
mulatto, but had means, and also a white woman
for a wife, and a family of five children. Not many
men of color left a slave state so well to do, and so
generally respected; but it was not in the nature
of things that he should be permitted to forget his
color. As we went along together, he riding a mule
and I on foot, he led the conversation to this
subject. He told me he should watch, when we got
to Oregon, what usage was awarded to people of
color, and if he could not have a free man's rights
he would seek the protection of the Mexican
Government in California or New Mexico. He
said there were few in that train he would say as
much to as he had just said to me. I told him I
understood. This conversation enabled me afterwards to understand the chief reason for Col.
M. T. Simmons and his kindred, and Bush and
Jones [a member of another family from Missouri
traveling with Bush] determining to settle north of
the Columbia River. It was understood that Bush
was assisting at least two of these to get to Oregon, and while they were all Americans, they
would take no part in ill treating G. W. Bush on
account of his color.*

The settlers in George Bush's wagon train were
true to their word, helping the Bush family overcome
the prejudice they encountered in Oregon territory.
Once the group was settled, in 1846, Michael Simmons
was elected to the legislature and undertook to exempt

Bush and his family from the antiblack laws in existence. In 1855, Simmons also asked Congress to grant Bush a homestead of 640 acres by special act. That land is now called Bush Prairie.

George W. Bush died in 1863, but his sons continued to work the homestead for which he and his friends had struggled. In 1891, his son, William Owen Bush, was elected to the state legislature. George W. Bush is remembered not only as the first black settler in the Oregon territories but, with his entire group, as the first Americans settling north of the Columbia River. Although Bush was a wealthy gentleman from Missouri, he had the determination and strength to face hardship and to lead his small band west into largely unexplored territory to make new lives in a new land.

Because there were few roads, nearly every early settler who headed west in the early 1800s was also an explorer, noting routes and landmarks, hazards and geography—information to pass on to those who followed after. Gradually, however, the frontier was pushed farther and farther west. As the United States entered the twentieth century, it seemed to many that there were no more frontiers to explore. Wherever there is the spirit of exploration, however, frontiers will be found—and so it has been throughout the twentieth century. The drive to know the unknown, seen in such explorers as Estevanico and George W. Bush has, in the twentieth century, moved men and women to explore the entire world . . . and beyond.

chapter
7

W hile the explorers of the American West faced many dangers in their travels, at least game and water were usually plentiful; and if winter with its cold and snow overtook them, they could, in time, expect warmth and spring. For Matthew Henson, in his explorations with Robert Peary at the North Pole, this was hardly the case. In many ways, to forge ahead into the icy Arctic took far greater stamina and courage than did the earlier explorers' travels, and Henson possessed such hardiness. As Donald MacMillan, a member of the expedition, was later to write: "Peary knew Matt Henson's real worth. . . . Highly respected by the Eskimos, he was easily the most popular man on board ship. . . . Henson . . . was of more real value to our Commander than [expedition members] Bartlett, Marvin, Borup, Goodsell and myself all put together. Matthew Henson went to the Pole with Peary because he was a better man than any one of us."

Matthew Henson was born on August 8, 1866, in Charles County, Maryland, some forty-four miles south of Washington, D.C. His parents were poor, free tenant farmers who barely eked a living from the sandy soil. The Civil War had ended the year before Matthew was born, bringing with it a great deal of bitterness on the part of former slaveowners. One manifestation of this hostility was the terrorist activity on the part of the Ku Klux Klan in Maryland. Many free and newly freed blacks had suffered at the hands of this band of night riders. Matthew's father, Lemuel Henson, felt it was only a matter of time before the Klan turned its vengeful eyes on his family. That, and the fact that by farming he was barely able to support them, caused him to decide to move north to Washington, D.C.

At first things went well for the Henson family, but then Matthew's mother died and his father found himself unable to care for Matthew. The seven-year-old boy was sent to live with his uncle, a kindly man who welcomed him and enrolled him in the N Street School. Six years later, however, another blow fell; his uncle himself fell upon hard times and could no longer support Matthew. The boy couldn't return to his father, because Lemuel had recently died. Alone, homeless, and penniless, Matthew was forced to fend for himself.

Matthew Henson was a bright boy and a hard worker, although he had only a sixth-grade education. Calling upon his own resourcefulness, he found a job as a dishwasher in a small restaurant owned by a woman named Janey Moore. When Janey discovered that Matthew had no place to stay, she fixed a cot for him in the kitchen; Matthew had found a home again.

Matthew Henson didn't want to spend his life waiting on people and washing dishes, however, no matter how kind Janey was. He had seen enough of the world through his schoolbooks to want more, to want adventure. This desire was reinforced by the men who frequented the restaurant—sailors from many ports, who spun tales of life on the ocean and of strange and wonderful places. As Henson listened, wide-eyed, to their stories, he decided, as had so many boys before him, that the life of a sailor with its adventures and dangers was for him. Having made up his mind, the fourteen-year-old packed up what little he owned, bade good-bye to Janey, and was off to Baltimore to find a ship.

Although Matthew Henson's early life seems harsh, in many ways he was very lucky. When he arrived in Baltimore, he signed on as a cabin boy on the *Katie Hines*, the master of which was a Captain Childs. For many sailors at that time, life at sea was brutal and filled with hard work, deprivation, and a "taste of the cat": whipping. The captains of many vessels were petty despots, ruling with an iron hand and having little regard for a seaman's health or safety. Matthew was fortunate to find just the opposite in Childs.

Captain Childs took the boy under his wing. Although Matthew of course had to do the work he was

assigned, Captain Childs took a fatherly interest in
him. Having an excellent private library on the ship,
the captain saw to Matthew's education, insisting that
he read widely in geography, history, mathematics, and
literature while they were at sea.

The years on the *Katie Hines* were good ones for
Matthew Henson. During that time he saw China,
Japan, the Philippines, France, Africa, and southern
Russia; he sailed through the Arctic to Murmansk. But
in 1885 it all ended; Captain Childs fell ill and died at
sea. Unable to face staying on the *Katie Hines* under a
new skipper, Matthew left the ship at Baltimore and
found a place on a fishing schooner bound for
Newfoundland.

Now, for the first time, Henson encountered the
kind of unthinking cruelty and tyranny so often found
on ships at that time. The ship was filthy, the crew surly
and resentful of their black shipmate, and the captain
a dictator. As soon as he was able, Matthew left the ship
in Canada and made his way back to the United States,
finally arriving in Washington, D.C., only to find that
things there had changed during the years he had been
at sea.

Opportunities for blacks had been limited when
Henson had left Washington in 1871, but by the time
he returned they were almost nonexistent. Post–Civil
War reconstruction had failed, bringing with its failure
a great deal of bitter resentment toward blacks. Jobs
were scarce and the few available were menial ones.
Matthew finally found a job as a stock clerk in a cloth-

ing and hat store, B. H. Steinmetz and Sons, bitterly wondering if this was how he was to spend the rest of his life. But his luck was still holding.

Steinmetz recognized that Matthew Henson was bright and hardworking. One day Lieutenant Robert E. Peary, a young navy officer, walked into the store, looking for tropical hats. After being shown a number of hats, Peary unexpectedly offered Henson a job as his personal servant. Steinmetz had recommended him, Peary said, but the job wouldn't be easy. He was bound for Nicaragua to head an engineering survey team. Would Matthew be willing to put up with the discomforts and hazards of such a trip? Thinking of the adventure and opportunities offered, Henson eagerly said yes, little realizing that a partnership had just been formed that would span years and be filled with exploration, danger, and fame.

Robert E. Peary was born in Cresson, Pennsylvania, in 1856, but was raised in Maine, where his mother had returned after his father's death in 1859. After graduating from Bowdoin College, Peary worked as a surveyor for four years and in 1881 joined the navy's corps of civil engineers. One result of his travels for the navy and of his reading was an ardent desire for adventure. "I shall not be satisfied," Peary wrote to his mother, "until my name is known from one end of the earth to the other." This was a goal Matthew Henson could understand. As he later said, "I recognized in [Peary] the qualities that made me willing to engage myself in his service." In November 1887, Henson and

Peary set sail for Nicaragua, along with forty-five other engineers and a hundred black Jamaicans.

Peary's job was to study the feasibility of digging a canal across Nicaragua (that canal that would later be dug across the Isthmus of Panama). The survey took until June of 1888, when the surveying party headed back to the United States. Henson knew he had done a good job for Peary, but, even as they started north, Peary said nothing to him about continuing on as his servant. It was a great surprise, then, when one day Peary approached Henson with a proposition. He wanted to try to raise money for an expedition to the Arctic, and he wanted Henson to accompany him. Henson quickly accepted, saying he would go whether Peary could pay him or not.

"It was in June, 1891, that I started on my first trip to the Arctic regions, as a member of what was known as the 'North Greenland Expedition,' " Matthew Henson later wrote. So began the first of five expeditions on which Henson would accompany Peary.

During this first trip to Greenland, on a ship named *Kite*, Peary discovered how valuable Henson was to any expedition. He reported that Henson was able to establish "a friendly relationship with the Eskimoes, who believed him to be somehow related to them because of his brown skin. . . ." Peary's expedition was also greatly aided by Henson's expert handling of the Eskimoes, dogs, and equipment. Henson also hunted with the Eskimos for meat for the expedition and cooked under the supervision of Josephine Peary,

*M*atthew Henson accompanied Robert Peary on several expeditions to find the North Pole and was with Peary when they finally accomplished their goal. But Peary did not publicly give credit to Henson. (Mary O'H. Williamson Collection, Prints and Photographs Department, Moorland—Spingarn Research Center, Howard University)

Robert's wife. On the expedition's return to New York, September 24, 1892, Peary wrote, "Henson, my faithful colored boy, a hard worker and apt at anything, . . . showed himself . . . the equal of others in the party."

This first expedition to the Arctic led to several others, but it was with the 1905 expedition that Peary first tried to find that mystical point, the North Pole, the sole goal of the 1908 expedition.

On July 6, 1908, the *Roosevelt* sailed from New York City. Aboard it were the supplies and men for an expedition to reach the North Pole. Accompanying Peary were Captain Robert Bartlett and Ross Martin, who had been with Peary on earlier expeditions; George Borup, a young graduate from Yale and the youngest member of the group; Donald MacMillan, a teacher; and a doctor, J. W. Goodsell. And, of course, Matthew Henson. In Greenland the group was joined by forty-one Eskimos and 246 dogs, plus the supplies. "The ship," Henson wrote, "is now in a most perfect state of dirtiness." On September 5, the *Roosevelt* arrived at Cape Sheridan and the group began preparing for their journey, moving supplies north to Cape Columbia by dog sled to establish a base camp. Peary named the camp Crane City in honor of Zenas Crane, who had contributed $10,000 to the expedition.

The plan was to have two men, Bartlett and Borup, go ahead of the rest of the group to cut a trail stretching from the base camp to the North Pole. On February 28, the two men set out, and on March 1, the remainder of the expedition started north, following the trail Bartlett and Borup had cut the day before. At first, trouble seemed to plague them. On the first day, three of the sledges broke, Henson's among them. Fortunately, Henson was able to repair them, despite the fact that it was nearly 50 degrees below zero.

As the days passed, further trouble came the way of the expedition. Several times they encountered leads—open channels of water—and were forced to wait until the ice closed over before proceeding. On March 14, Peary decided to send Donald MacMillan and Dr. Goodsell back to the base camp. MacMillan could hardly walk, because he had frozen a heel when his foot had slipped into one of the leads. Dr. Goodsell was exhausted. As the expedition went on, more men were sent back due to exhaustion and frostbite. George Borup was sent back on March 20, and, on the 26th, so was Ross Marvin.

Although the expedition had encountered problems with subzero temperatures, with open water, and in handling the dogs, they had had no real injuries. On Ross Marvin's return trip to the base camp, however, he met with tragedy. On his journey, Marvin was accompanied by two Eskimos. He told them that he would go ahead to scout the trail. About an hour later, the Eskimos came upon a hole in the ice; floating in it was Marvin's coat. Marvin had gone through thin ice and, unable to save himself, had drowned or frozen. The Peary expedition had suffered its first—and fortunately its last—fatality.

By April 1, Peary had sent back all of the original expedition except for four Eskimos and Matthew Henson. When Bartlett, the last man to be sent back, asked

Peary why he didn't also send Henson, Peary replied, "I can't get along without him." The remnant of the original group pushed on.

> *We had been travelling eighteen to twenty hours out of every twenty-four. Man, that was killing work! Forced marches all the time. From all our other expeditions we had found out that we couldn't carry food for more than fifty days, fifty-five at a pinch. . . .*
>
> *We used to travel by night and sleep in the warmest part of the day. I was ahead most of the time with two of the Eskimos.*

So Matthew Henson described the grueling journey. Finally, on the morning of April 6, Peary called a halt. Henson wrote: "I was driving ahead and was swinging around to the right. . . . The Commander, who was about 50 feet behind me, called to me and said we would go into camp. . . ." In fact, both Henson and Peary felt they might have reached the Pole already. That day, Peary took readings with a sextant and determined that they were within three miles of the Pole. Later he sledged ten miles north and found he was traveling south; to return to camp, Peary would have to return north and then head south in another direction—something that could only happen at the North Pole. To be absolutely sure, the next day Peary again took readings from solar observations. It was the North Pole, he was sure.

On that day Robert Peary had Matthew Henson plant the American flag at the North Pole. Peary then cut a piece from the flag and placed it and two letters in a glass jar that he left at the Pole. The letters read:

> *90 N. Lat., North Pole*
> *April 6, 1909*
>
> *Arrived here today, 27 marches from C. Columbia.*
>
> *I have with me 5 men, Matthew Henson, colored, Ootah, Egingwah, Seegloo, and Ooqueah, Eskimos; 5 sledges and 38 dogs. My ship, the S.S.* Roosevelt, *is in winter quarters at Cape Sheridan, 90 miles east of Columbia.*
>
> *The expedition under my command which has succeeded in reaching the Pole is under the auspices of the Peary Arctic Club of New York City, and has been fitted out and sent north by members and friends of the Club for the purpose of securing this geographical prize, if possible, for the honor and prestige of the United States of America.*
>
> *The officers of the Club are Thomas H. Hubbard of New York, President; Zenas Crane, of Mass., Vice-president; Herbert L. Bridgman, of New York, Secretary and Treasurer.*
>
> *I start back for Cape Columbia tomorrow.*
>
> *Robert E. Peary*
> *United States Navy*
>
> *90 No. Lat., North Pole*
> *April 6, 1909*
>
> *I have today hoisted the national ensign of the United States of America at this place, which my observations indicate to be the North Polar*

axis of the earth, and have formally taken posses-
sion of the entire region, and adjacent, for and in
the name of the President of the United States of
America.
    I leave this record and United States flag in
possession.

               Robert E. Peary
               United States Navy

    Having accomplished their goal, the small group set out on the return journey. It was, Matthew Henson wrote, "17 days of haste, toil, and misery. . . . We crossed lead after lead, sometimes like a bareback rider in the circus, balancing on cake after cake of ice." Finally they reached the *Roosevelt*, where they could rest and eat well at last. The Pole had been conquered!

    During the return trip to New York City, Henson became increasingly puzzled by Peary's behavior. "Not once in [three weeks]," Henson wrote, "did he speak a word to me. Then he . . . ordered me to get to work. Not a word about the North Pole or anything connected with it." Even when the *Roosevelt* docked in New York in September of 1909, Peary remained withdrawn and silent, saying little to the press and quickly withdrawing to his home in Maine.

    The ostensible reason for his silence was that when the group returned to New York, they learned that Dr. Frederick A. Cook was claiming that *he* had gone to the North Pole—and done so before Peary reached it. Peary told his friends that he wished to wait for his own proofs to be validated by the scientific societies before he spoke. He felt sure that Cook would not be able to present the kinds of evidence that he could present, and so it proved.

On December 15, Peary was declared the first to reach the North Pole; Cook could not present adequate evidence that he had made the discovery. Peary and Bartlett were awarded gold medals by the National Geographic Society; Henson was not. Because Henson was black, his contributions to the expedition were not recognized for many years.

After 1909, Henson worked in a variety of jobs. For a while, he was a parking-garage attendant in Brooklyn and, at the age of forty-six, he became a clerk in the U.S. Customs House in Lower Manhattan. In the meantime, friends tried again and again to have his contributions to the expedition recognized. At last, in 1937, nearly thirty years after the expedition, he was invited to join the Explorers Club in New York, and, in 1944, Congress authorized a medal for all of the men on the expedition, including Matthew Henson.

After his death in New York City on March 9, 1955, another lasting tribute was made to Henson's endeavors. In 1961, his home state of Maryland placed a bronze tablet in memory of him in the State House. It reads, in part:

MATTHEW ALEXANDER HENSON
Co-Discoverer of the North Pole
with
Admiral Robert Edwin Peary
April 6, 1909

MATTHEW ALEXANDER HENSON
CO-DISCOVERER OF THE NORTH POLE
WITH
ADMIRAL ROBERT EDWIN PEARY
APRIL 6, 1909
* * * * * *
BORN: AUGUST 8, 1866   DIED: MARCH 9, 1955

SON OF MARYLAND
EXEMPLIFICATION OF COURAGE, FORTITUDE AND PATRIOTISM,
WHOSE VALIANT DEEDS OF NOBLE DEVOTION
UNDER THE COMMAND OF ADMIRAL ROBERT EDWIN PEARY,
IN PIONEER ARCTIC EXPLORATION AND DISCOVERY,
ESTABLISHED EVERLASTING PRESTIGE AND GLORY
FOR HIS STATE AND COUNTRY

BY THE STATE OF MARYLAND
J. MILLARD TAWES, GOVERNOR
THE BOARD OF PUBLIC WORKS
J. MILLARD TAWES   GOVERNOR
LOUIS L. GOLDSTEIN   COMPTROLLER
HOOPER S. MILES   TREASURER
ANDREW KRUSECK, JR.   SECRETARY

THE GOVERNOR'S ADVISORY COMMITTEE
HERBERT M. FRISBY, CHAIRMAN   MRS. J. WILLIAM MIDDENDORF, JR.
SENATOR J. ALVIN JONES   ALBERT P. BACKHAUS

*N*ot until 1961, six years after his death and fifty-two years after his codiscovery of the North Pole, was Matthew Henson honored by his home state of Maryland for his accomplishment. (Mary O'H. Williamson Collection, Prints and Photographs Department, Moorland—Spingarn Research Center, Howard University)

*Son of Maryland, exemplification of courage,
fortitude and patriotism, whose valiant deeds of
noble devotion under the command of Admiral
Robert Edwin Peary, in pioneer arctic exploration
and discovery, established everlasting prestige
and glory for his State and Country. . . .*

In 1986 S. Allen Counter, a professor of neuro-
science at Harvard University, decided to investigate
persistent rumors of "dark-skinned" Eskimos in north-
western Greenland. He traveled there and found Anaukaq, Matthew Henson's son and his only child, and
Anaukaq's family. Henson was remembered fondly by
the Inuit, whose nickname for him means "Matthew
the Kind One."

Anaukaq then led Counter to a "white-skinned"
Eskimo named Kali, the son of Robert Peary. Kali was
not as eager to talk about his father as Anaukaq was
about his, for Kali said Peary had not helped him or his
mother in any way.

Counter arranged for both Anaukaq and Kali and
their families to visit their American relatives in 1987.
The American Pearys refused to have anything to do
with the American-Inuit Pearys and would not attend a
ceremony in their honor. Eventually, Robert Peary, Jr.,
and his family greeted Kali briefly at their home in
Maine.

Anauqak had a happier experience. The American
Hensons, descendants of Matthew's siblings, were
proud of their newly discovered relatives and welcomed

them warmly. Anauqak died shortly after his return home, but he died happy, for family continuity was important to him, and he had finally seen his American relatives.

chapter 8

THE STARS,
MY GOAL:
GUION STEWART
BLUFORD, JR.

As the twentieth century progressed, humankind turned its eyes to the unexplored expanse of outer space. While small discoveries were continually being made about our home planet, the earth, the frontier to be explored now stretched beyond the planet and spread to the stars. The 1960s saw years of effort to break the bonds of gravity, effort that had begun with the launching of *Sputnik I* by the Soviet Union in 1957. Inspired by that launching and the concomitant interest in a space program in the United States, a young black high school student, Guion Stewart (Guy) Bluford, Jr., also turned his eyes to the stars.

Guy Bluford was born on November 22, 1942, in Philadelphia, Pennsylvania. His mother was a teacher

of special education and his father a mechanical engineer. Even as a baby Guy took after his father, showing
an interest in mechanical things. He wanted to know
how they worked. Guy had lots of mechanical toys
to take apart, . . . but what he liked best were things
that flew.

That interest was to fill his childhood. His room
was filled with airplane models and pictures of air-
planes. His interest wasn't so much in flying them, but
in designing them. He was fascinated with the way they
were put together, why they flew. His father encouraged this curiosity and made his many engineering
books available to Guy. Guy knew very early that he
wanted to be an aerospace engineer. Guy knew he
wanted to design, build, and fly spacecraft, and when
he was fifteen and *Sputnik I* was launched, his dreams
became even more real.

In the late 1950s, just as the days of the civil rights
movement were beginning, the idea of a black man
becoming an aerospace engineer was barely conceiva-
ble to many people. Although encouraged at home,
Guy didn't receive that same encouragement at school.
His high school guidance counselor didn't urge him
to pursue his goal and go to college; in fact, he was told
that he wasn't college material. He was told that he
should aim for a technical school or learn a mechanical
trade. However, he says,

> *I really wasn't too concerned about what that*
> *counselor said. I just ignored it. I'm pretty sure*
> *that all of us have had times when somebody told*

*us we couldn't do this or shouldn't do that. I
had such a strong interest in aerospace engineering by then that nothing a counselor said was
going to stop me.*

In the fall of 1960, Guy started college at Pennsylvania State University, in the aerospace engineering
program. In addition to his regular studies, Guy also
joined the air force Reserve Officers Training Corps
(ROTC), hoping to become a pilot. In his junior year,
however, he failed a physical and couldn't qualify as
a pilot. During ROTC summer camp that year, he at
least passed the flight physical—and got his first ride in
an air force T-33 plane. "I changed directions right
then and there," he said. "I decided to go into the Air
Force as a pilot. I thought that if I were a pilot, I would
be a better engineer." During his senior year at Penn
State, Guy flew as a pilot in the air force ROTC and,
upon graduation, received the ROTC's Distinguished
Graduate Award.

While at Penn State, Guy had met and married
Linda Tull, a fellow student; after graduation he joined
the air force, moving to Arizona with his wife and new
son, Guion III, who had been born in June of 1964.
His second son, James Trevor, was born in 1965, just at
the time the Vietnam War was becoming an important
factor in the lives of many Americans.

For the next several years, Guy saw little of his
family. As pilot of an F-4C fighter plane, he was assigned to the 557th Tactical Fighter Squadron, based in
Cam Ranh Bay, South Vietnam. During his tour of

duty he flew 144 combat missions and received ten air force medals. But he had not forgotten his goal of becoming an aerospace engineer and flying in outer space.

When Guy returned to the United States, he applied to the Air Force Institute of Technology, receiving a master's degree in 1974 and, in 1978, a Ph.D. in aerospace engineering. His doctoral thesis was entitled "A Numerical Solution of Supersonic and Hypersonic Viscous Flow Fields Around Thin Planar Delta Wings." As he explains:

> *Delta wings are triangular wings. I calculated how the air goes around the wings at speeds greater than the speed of sound—three to four times the speed of sound and faster. If you had picked a place anywhere along a wing, I could have told you what the pressure, the density, and the velocity of the air was above and below that place. I developed a computer program that could do that.*

The same year Guy received his Ph.D., he applied to enter the astronaut training program at NASA (the National Aeronautics and Space Administration). NASA seemed, to Guy, to be the ideal place to put both his engineering and piloting skills to use, although he wasn't sure if he would be accepted. In 1978 alone, 8,878 other people had applied for the program. A few weeks later, however, he learned that he had been accepted. It was the fulfillment of a dream. Bluford and his family quickly moved to Houston, where he began his training.

The astronaut training program lasted a year and involved studying subjects such as shuttle systems, geology, medicine, aerodynamics, communications, and astronomy. It also involved a great deal of travel.

We went to a lot of the NASA space centers, including Kennedy Space Center at Cape Canaveral, Florida; Marshall Space Center in Huntsville, Alabama, where they develop the engines; and Rockwell Aircraft Company on the West Coast, where they build the shuttles. We traveled around the country, meeting all of the people associated with the shuttle program.

By 1979, Guy Bluford was a full-fledged astronaut, qualified to go into space. He spent the next several years in further training, flying the "shuttle simulators" in both Houston and California, hoping and waiting, as were all the astronauts, to be chosen for that special ride beyond the skies of earth.

The shuttle program had begun in 1972, three years after Neil Armstrong and Edwin Aldrin had taken their historic walk on the moon. After the moon landing, interest in the space program had waned somewhat. The 1970s were full of problems here on earth that diverted public interest: the Watergate scandals of the Nixon administration, the Vietnam War, and rising inflation in the economy. One reason NASA began the shuttle program was to save money. The shuttle, unlike earlier rockets, was reusable. More versatile than the earlier rockets, it served not only as transportation, but also as a laboratory and living

Guion Stewart Bluford, Jr., was the first black American astronaut in space. In 1983 he flew as a mission specialist on the space shuttle Challenger. *(National Aeronautics and Space Administration)*

quarters. It could carry many things into space and was, compared to the rockets, much larger.

The first space shuttle, *Columbia,* was launched in April of 1981. The second shuttle, *Challenger,* went into service in 1983. On its second flight—two months before the flight Guy Bluford would be on—one of three mission specialists was Dr. Sally Ride, the first American woman in space.

Guy Bluford did not want to be known as merely a "black astronaut": he wanted to be known as a man who did a good job. All of the astronauts shared this view. As Sally Ride said about all the publicity her flight had generated, "I didn't go into the space program to make money or be famous." In 1983, when Guy was told that he was scheduled for the next *Challenger* flight, he was exhilarated—not to be the first black American in space, but because, finally, he would be doing what he had dreamed of all his life: putting *all* his skills to use.

On August 30, 1983, thunderstorms had swept across the sandy expanse of Cape Canaveral, Florida, but the air was now clear. In the hot, damp night, the *Challenger* stood over five stories high on launch pad 39-A. It was lighted both from above, by lights on the gantry, and from below, as this would be the first night-time launch since *Apollo 17* in 1972.

The five men inside the *Challenger* were busy checking equipment, listening to the hollow voice of mission control as the final countdown proceeded. Aboard were thirty-four-year-old Dale Gardner, a navy fighter pilot and engineer; Dr. William Thornton, at fifty-four the oldest person to fly in space; Richard Truly, a Vietnam War veteran and test pilot, who would serve as commander of the shuttle; thirty-nine-year-old Daniel Brandenstein, a navy commander; and Guion Bluford, Jr., who would serve as mission specialist. Guy was in charge of the experiments the crew were to conduct during the flight.

Just before lift-off, the crew received a message from President Ronald Reagan. "With this effort," he said, "we acknowledge proudly the first ascent of a black American into space." But Guy wasn't thinking of that; he was thinking of the flight. He was eager, curious, and excited, but not afraid: "We'd spent so much time training for the mission and riding in shuttle simulators that we were pretty well prepared. It's like preparing for an exam. You study as much as you can, and the better prepared you are, the less frightened you are about taking the exam."

At 2:32 A.M., August 30, 1983, fire blazed from the rockets and lit up the Florida landscape. As Richard Truly described it, "It got brighter and brighter. When the boosters separated it was 500 times brighter than I remember [from past launches]." Dale Gardner tried to twist around for a better view; "I damn near blinded myself," he said later. The brightness of the rockets' flare surprised all of the men.

"But otherwise, there weren't any surprises," Guy said. "What amazed me was that the shuttle flew just like the simulator said it was going to fly. The only differences were the motion, the vibration, and the noise. You don't get those in simulators. When I felt the movement and heard the noise, I thought, Hey, this thing really does take off and roar!"

Once in orbit, Bluford began to operate one of the main experiments, an electrophoresis system designed to separate living cells, aimed at one day producing new medical advances. It was difficult, initially, to work in weightlessness, but also exhilarating. Although all the men had trained for weightlessness in a water-immersion tank, it was still a new sensation. But everything was new and exciting. Circling the earth every ninety minutes, the crew slept, ate, and did their work in that new frontier—space.

On September 5, the shuttle glided to a perfect landing back on earth, at Edwards Air Force Base in California. Only later did NASA reveal that the crew had been in danger: The lining of a solid fuel booster's nozzle had almost burned through during launching. Such an accident would have thrown the shuttle wildly off course, causing it to crash. Fourteen seconds—the time it would have taken for the lining to burn all the way through—was all that had separated the crew and shuttle from disaster.

All who venture to explore the unknown recognize the threat of disaster. This possibility doesn't stop them, however; risk is part of the job. So is determination. Throughout his life, Guion Bluford had one goal in mind—to work and fly in space, and he was determined to let nothing get in the way of achieving that goal. As he has said, it was "difficult at times—I had to struggle through those courses at Penn State—but if you really want to do something and are willing to put in the hard work it takes, then someday—bingo, you've done it!" With this kind of stick-to-itiveness, it isn't surprising that Guy Bluford became the first black American explorer of space.

chapter 9

RONALD McNAIR

AND THE CHALLENGER

DISASTER

Although Guion Bluford was the first black American to go into space, he was not the first black astronaut. Nearly two decades before, in 1962, air force captain Edward Dwight had joined the astronaut training program. At the time, the United States was immersed in the space program; in 1961 Alan Shepard had become America's first man in space, bursting beyond earth's atmosphere in the *Freedom 7*. But in 1966, embittered, Edward Dwight left the program. His leaving was due to what he believed to be pressure from NASA officials. "They didn't want black involvement," he later said. "They felt that to send blacks into space would lessen the general public's enthusiasm for the space program."

The second black astronaut to enter the training program was Robert Lawrence. He was appointed to the program by President Lyndon Johnson shortly after President John F. Kennedy's assassination. Tragically, Lawrence died in a plane crash soon after his appointment.

After Lawrence's death little active effort was made to recruit blacks into the space program. However, by the 1970s attitudes at NASA had changed, and in 1978 when Guy Bluford joined the astronaut training program he was accompanied by two other black men: Colonel Frederick D. Gregory and Ronald E. McNair.

Ronald McNair was twenty-eight years old when he joined the astronaut training program. Much of his life he had dreamed of going into space and of using his knowledge in the unique conditions of outer space. Born in 1950, in Lake City, South Carolina, McNair was fortunate to have parents who were supportive of his dreams, encouraging him to get a good education, and reinforcing him in his faith.

After high school, Ronald McNair started to pursue his dreams in earnest, graduating from North Carolina A & T University with a bachelor of science degree in physics. He then went on to the Massachusetts Institute of Technology where he received his Ph.D., also in physics. Ronald then worked in the area of ocular physics, presenting papers both in the United States and in Europe on lasers and on molecular spectroscopy. He also applied to NASA for the astronaut training program. In 1978, the same year his alma mater, North Carolina A & T, presented him with an honorary doctorate of laws, he was accepted into the astronaut program.

Ronald McNair began his training with Guy Bluford in January of 1978. Both were trained as mission specialists. In 1983, when the crews were scheduled, McNair was disappointed that Bluford rather than he had been chosen to be the first black American in space, but, as Bluford said, "The three of us never talk about my being first. We all recognize that somebody has to play this role, just as one of the women had to be first." McNair's first voyage into space was set for early 1984.

On February 3, 1984, the shuttle *Challenger* lifted off from Cape Canaveral with a crew of five: Vance Brand, Bruce McCandless, Edward Gibson, Robert Stewart, and Ronald McNair. The most important part of their mission, the deployment of two communications satellites, was a failure. Plagued with hardware problems, the booster rockets on the satellites misfired, sending them tumbling uselessly into space.

The second part of their mission proved more successful. On February 7, Bruce McCandless and Robert Stewart took a historic six-hour space walk, the longest yet made. One purpose of the walk was to test an astronaut-manned maneuvering unit (MMU) that had been developed by McCandless. McCandless was elated: The MMU worked! Propelled into space, he radioed, "That may have been one small step for Neil [Armstrong], but it was a heck of a big leap for me."

What was Ronald McNair doing during all this

time? His job as mission specialist was to work the space shuttle's "arm," a cranelike device used to lift astronauts and equipment in space. While McCandless and Stewart tested the MMU, McNair was busy maneuvering and monitoring a TV camera that was mounted on the arm, recording the maneuvers of the two "space walkers."

McNair's own testing of equipment came at the end of that walk when McCandless placed his feet in a restraint at the arm's end. With McNair moving the arm, the two practiced satellite repairs, after which McNair lifted McCandless around to the cargo bay. Although McNair had practiced often on the simulator during training on earth, conditions in space were very different. The procedure went smoothly, however, and he was delighted. Unfortunately, the next day an electrical problem developed in the arm's "wrist joint," so further arm maneuvers had to be scratched.

On February 11, Brand landed the *Challenger* back at Cape Canaveral, the first shuttle landing to be made in Florida. Despite the problems that had occurred during the flight, the mission was considered a success, and Ronald McNair was now a veteran of space. However, McNair was to wait almost two years to the day for his next shuttle mission.

January 28, 1986, was clear, bright—and cold for Florida, nearly freezing. On the launch pad the *Challenger* towered over the flat Florida landscape like a skyscraper, ready for its tenth mission in space. While other shuttle missions had come and gone almost unnoticed by the American public, who were blasé about them now, this mission was special. For the first time a private citizen, school teacher Christa McAuliffe, thirty-seven, would accompany the professional astronauts into space. The entire nation was watching.

Another reason why the mission was special was that the seven-member crew was, for the first time, really representative of the American people. On the mission also were air force major Ellison Onizuka, the first Asian-American in space, who had been a flight test engineer at Edwards Air Force Base before joining NASA; Judith Resnik, thirty-six, a classical pianist with a Ph.D. in electrical engineering, who had been the second woman in space; Gregory Jarvis, forty-one, who was not an astronaut but was with the flight as the payload engineer in charge of the Tracking and Data Relay Satellite (TDRS) that was to be launched during the mission; and Ronald McNair, who was thirty-six years old and the father of two young sons. Commanding the mission was Francis Scobee, forty-six, a Vietnam War veteran and a former test pilot. Scobee's pilot was navy commander Michael Smith. Smith was also a Vietnam War veteran, with a master's degree in aeronautical engineering; this was to be his first flight.

During the previous months, both Gregory Jarvis and Christa McAuliffe had undergone training for the mission. Their training, however, was not as intense or technical as that of the astronauts. It consisted of little more than an orientation and training in how to live and work in the shuttle.

The mission of the *Challenger* on this flight was to launch the TDRS, a communications satellite, and to study Halley's comet. The shuttle had originally been scheduled for lift-off on January 22 but had been plagued by bad weather and mechanical problems that caused delay after delay. Finally, on January 28, officials felt that conditions were right, although the temperature overnight had been well below freezing. Icicles had formed on the launch pad and shuttle, and the engineers were concerned that they would fall and damage the tiles that covered the outside of the shuttle. Later, the engineers would say that they worried that the cold would also affect the efficiency of the O-ring seals on the solid fuel rocket boosters.

Those at Cape Canaveral who had come to watch the launch were bundled up against the cold. Meanwhile, teams went out three times to the launch pad to clear ice away. Later, when the crew had taken their places in the shuttle, the following conversation occurred:

> JUDITH RESNIK: Is that snow?
> FRANCIS SCOBEE: Yep, that's snow. [Frost was blowing off the external tanks.]
> RONALD MCNAIR: You're kidding. You see snow on the window?

After settling into their seats in the shuttle, the crewmembers in turn checked their communications hookups and tested the cabin pressure. Then the waiting began. Finally, at 11:38 Eastern Standard Time, *Challenger* rose to meet the sky. The following was heard by mission control as the shuttle lifted off:

JUDITH RESNIK: Aaall right!
MICHAEL SMITH: Here we go!

Relieved to have taken off at last after so many problems and delays, the crew performed their work flawlessly, occasionally making excited comments. But, at T plus one minute and thirteen seconds, Mission Control heard the last sound to come from the *Challenger*, when a crew member suddenly said, "Uhh . . . oh!"

What the watchers below saw was terrifying and incomprehensible. Suddenly, the twin solid rocket boosters began flying away from the moving clouds of smoke and fire, leaving fiery trails in their wake. Flame and smoke filled the sunlit sky where minutes before the *Challenger* had risen on a pedestal of vapor. Explosions rocked the air and, instead of the shuttle, a fireball filled the sky. The *Challenger* and its brave crew of space explorers were gone.

The nation mourned along with the families of the astronauts. Although disaster had struck the space program once before, the *Challenger* was different because of all the lives lost and of the special quality of the mission. All the members of the crew will be remembered as special pioneers who dared to go beyond the known into the unknown.

On January 31, 1986, a memorial service was held for the *Challenger* crew at the Johnson Space Center in Houston, Texas. In his eulogy, President Ronald Reagan said,

We remember Dick Scobee, the commander, who
spoke the last words we heard from the space

shuttle Challenger. *We remember Michael
Smith, who earned enough medals as a combat
pilot to cover his chest. We remember Judith
Resnik, known as J. R. to her friends. We remember Ellison Onizuka who, as a child running
barefoot through the coffee fields and macadamia
groves of Hawaii, dreamed of someday traveling
to the Moon. We remember Ronald McNair
who said he learned perseverance in the cotton
fields of South Carolina. . . .*

And the *Challenger* crew *is* remembered, both in
the minds of Americans and in the continuing exploration of space. As V. June Scobee-Rodgers, widow of
Francis Scobee, said, "The *Challenger* crew wouldn't
want a bricks-and-mortar memorial. They'd want us to
carry on their mission to explore space and to teach."

Ronald McNair knew there were risks involved in
being an astronaut; there are always risks when one
dares to approach the unknown. But he also had
known, as Matthew Henson had earlier written, that
"the path is not easy, the climbing is rugged and hard,
but the glory at the end is worthwhile. . . ."

R onald McNair flew safely in Challenger *in February 1984. But two years later he was one of a crew of seven, among them teacher Christa McAuliffe, who died in the tragic explosion of* Challenger. *(National Aeronautics and Space Administration)*

afterword

*F*rontiers are not just geographic or stellar
boundaries. Frontiers exist in every area of
knowledge. The scientist finding a cure for a
disease has just stepped beyond the frontiers of his or
her field to plant the flag of discovery in as real a way
as the explorer of the outer world.

In the years and decades to come, humankind's
frontiers will stretch farther and farther—from the
planets and beyond the sun, to the microscopic world
that surrounds us unseen. And, as has been the case
since before recorded time, black men and women will
be there to share the glory of discovery. But in many
ways, these explorers go forth not for glory; rather,
they have a vision of the world, a vision of discovery. As
Anne Devereaux Jordan put it in "Farewell and Then
Forever," *Isaac Asimov's Science Fiction Magazine,* February 1983,

> *I will go. Not because I will be forgotten*
> *Or remembered*

Or revered.

. . .

I will go because I share a hope in waiting stars,
New worlds, beginnings wrought from this end.

bibliography

Adams, Russell L. *Great Negroes Past and Present*. 3rd ed. Chicago: Afro-Am Publishing Co., 1969.

Bergman, Peter M. *The Chronological History of the Negro in America*. New York: Harper & Row, 1969.

Bond, Peter. *Heroes in Space, From Gagarin to* Challenger. Oxford, England: Basil Blackwell, 1987.

Bradley, Michael. *The Black Discovery of America*. Toronto: Personal Library, 1981.

Colon, Ferdinand. *Life of Admiral Christopher Columbus*, trans. B. Keen. London: Greenwood Press, 1978.

Davidson, Basil. *The Lost Cities of Africa*. Boston: Little, Brown & Co., 1959.

Dolan, Edward F., Jr. *Matthew Henson, Black Explorer*. New York: Dodd, Mead, 1979.

Encyclopedia of Discovery and Exploration: The Conquest of North America. Garden City, N.Y.: Doubleday & Co., 1971.

Ferris, Jeri. *Arctic Explorer: The Story of Matthew Henson*. Minneapolis: Carolrhoda Books, 1989.

Hakluyt, Richard. *Hakluyt's Collection of the Early Voyages, Travels, and Discoveries of the English Nation*. London, 1810.

Haskins, James & Kathleen Benson. *Space Challenger, The Story of Guion Bluford*. Minneapolis: Carolrhoda Books, 1984.

Hughes, Langston. *Famous Negro Heroes of America.* New York: Dodd, Mead, 1958.

Katz, William Loren. *The Black West.* Seattle: Open Hand Publishing, 1973.

————. *Eyewitness: The Negro in American History.* New York: Pitman Publishing, 1967.

Lavender, David. *The Way to the Western Sea.* New York: Harper & Row, 1988.

Lecture Notes of Matthew A. Henson. Henson Collection, Soper Library, Morgan State College, Baltimore.

Lewis, Richard S. *Challenger, The Final Voyage.* New York: Columbia University Press, 1988.

Ploski, Harry A. and James Williams. *The Negro Almanac.* Detroit: Gale Research, 1989.

Ripley, Sheldon N. *Matthew Henson, Arctic Hero.* Boston: Houghton Mifflin Co., 1966.

index

Page numbers in italics refer to illustrations.

Abulfeda, 3
African civilizations, 2–3, 6, 8
African exploration of New World, 3–6
Africanus, Leo, 8
Aldrin, Edwin, 66
Anaukaq (son of M. Henson), 60–61
Armstrong, Neil, 66, 74
Ashley, William Henry, 32, 33
Astronauts, black, 62–71, 72–80

Bartlett, Robert, 47, 53, 54–55, 58
Beckwourth, James P., 31–39, *34*, 41
Beckwourth Pass, 36–39, *37*
Blackfoot Indians, 33–36
Blacks
  contributions of, 2, 39, 58
  in exploration/discovery, 2, 30, 40–45, 81
  and Indians, 11, 18, 23, 26–27, 32–36, 41
  post-Civil War, 49
Bluford, Guion Stewart (Guy), Jr., 2, 62–71, *67*, 72, 73, 74
Borup, George, 47, 53–54
Brand, Vance, 74, 75
Brandenstein, Daniel, 69
Bush, George W., 52–55
Bush, William Owen, 45

Cape Canaveral, 75, 77
Challenger (space shuttle), 68–70, 74–79
Cheyenne-Arapaho War, 39
Chicago, founding of, 15–23
Childs, Captain, 48–49
Civil War, 40, 42, 47
Clark, William, 25–30
Clemorgan, Jacques, 16, 17–18
Clinch, Colonel, 41

Colon, Ferdinand, 4–6
Columbia (space shuttle), 68
Columbus, Christopher, 4–6, 8
Cook, Frederick A., 57–58
Counter, S. Allen, 60
Crane, Zenas, 53
Crow Indians, 33–36, 39

de Vaco, Alvar Núñez Cabeza, 10
Dorantez de Carranze, Andres, 9
Dorion, Paul, 35–36
Dwight, Edward, 72

Eskimos, 46, 51, 53, 56, 60–61
Estevanico (Stephan Dorantez, "Little Stephen"), 2, 7–14, 45
Exploration
  blacks in, 8–9, 30, 40–45, 81
  see also Space exploration
Explorers, New World, 2–6, 40–45
Eyewitness (Katz), 39

"Farewell and Then Forever" (Jordan), 81–82
Florida, 9–10, 41–42
Florida Indians, 9
Freedom 7 (spacecraft), 72
Frémont, John C., 36–37
French and Indian Wars, 18
Frontier, 45, 62, 81

Gardner, Dale, 68–69
Gibson, Edward, 74
Goodsell, J. W., 47, 53–54
Gregory, Frederick D., 73

Hakluyt, Richard, 14
Henson, Matthew, 1–2, 46–61, *52*, *59*, 79
Hudson Bay Company, 42
Hughes, Langston, 8

Ibn Amir Hajib, 3–4
Indians, 11, 18, 23, 26–27, 32–36

Jackson, Andrew, 43
Jarvis, Gregory, 76
Jefferson, Thomas, 24, 30
Jesup, Thomas, 42
Johnson, Lyndon, 73
Jordan, Anne Devereaux, 81–82

Kali (son of R. Peary), 60
Katz, William, 39
Kearny, Stephen, 36
Kennedy, John F., 73
Kinzie, John, 22
Ku Klux Klan, 47

Lalime, John, 21
Lawrence, Robert, 73
Lewis, Meriwether, 24–30
Lewis and Clark Expedition, 24–30, 31

McAuliffe, Christa, 76
McCandless, Bruce, 74, 75
MacMillan, Donald, 46–47, 53–54
NcNair, Ronald E., 72–80, *80*
Mali, emperor of, 2–4, 8
Marvin, Ross, 47, 53–54
Masakil-al-absub (Omari), 3
Mendoza, Antonio de, 10
Minton, John, 43–44
Missouri Compromise, 43
Missouri River, 24–25, 29, 30
Moore, Janey, 48
Musa, Kankum, emperor of Mali, 3–4

Narváez, Pánfile de, 9
NASA, 65, 66, 70, 72, 73
New Orleans, 17, 32
New World, 2–6, 7, 8–9
Niño, Pedro Alonzo, 6
Niza, Fray Marcos de, 10–14
North America, 40–45
North Greenland Expedition, 51–53
North Pole, 2, 53–61

Omari, 3
Onizuka, Ellison, 76, 79
Oregon territory, 42–45

Pacific Ocean, 24–25, 29–30
Peary, Josephine, 51–53
Peary, Robert, 46–61
Peary, Robert, Jr., 60
Point du Sable, Jean Baptiste, 16–23, *20*, 32

Reagan, Ronald, 69, 78–79
Resnik, Judith, 76–78, 79
Ride, Sally, 68
Risk, 70, 79

Sacajawea, 26
Scobee, Francis, 76, 77, 78–79
Seminole Indians, 41–42
Seminole Wars, 36, 41–42
Seven Cities of Cíbola, 10–14
Shepard, Alan, 72
Sherman, William Tecumseh, 32
Shuttle program, 66–68
Sierra Nevada Mountains, 36–38, 39
Simmons, Michael T., 43, 44–45
Slavery, slave trade, 7–8
    destruction of African civilizations by, 2, 6, 8
    U.S., 17, 31, 32, 42, 43
Slaves, 9, 15
Smith, Michael, 76, 78, 79
Songhay (empire, Africa), 8
Space exploration, 62
Sputnik I (spacecraft), 62, 63
Steinmetz, B. H., 50
Stevenson, James, 32–33
Stewart, Robert, 74, 75

Thornton, William, 68–69
Trapping, trading, 15–16
    by blacks (U.S.), 17–18, 21, 32–33
Truly, Richard, 69

Vietnam War, 64–65, 66

York (slave of W. Clark), 26–30, *28*